T0064729

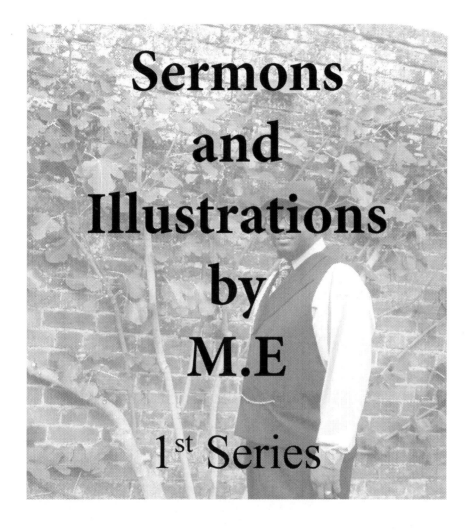

Sermons
and
Illustrations
by
M.E

1st Series

Compiled, Revised and Built by: M.E. Lyons

authorHOUSE®

AuthorHouse™
1663 Liberty Drive
Bloomington, IN 47403
www.authorhouse.com
Phone: 1-800-839-8640

Published by AuthorHouse   02/21/2013

ISBN: 978-1-4817-1703-8 (sc)
ISBN: 978-1-4817-1701-4 (hc)
ISBN: 978-1-4817-1702-1 (e)

Library of Congress Control Number: 2013902701

Contents

General Illustrations

Funeral Illustrations

What's On Your Mind?

Isaiah 26:3

The greatest tragedy of our time is that of satan playing with our mind
(Garden of Eden)

What plagues our land is the problems that originate in our minds many times begin to lodge in our minds

Our minds are sensitive to what is taking place around us

It is the processor of human emotions

It tells us how to think, feel, react and often control our senses

It can be deceived but it also can be deceptive, that's why one song writer says in the secular world: "Your mind's playing tricks on you"

So I have a simple question for you tonight

"What's on your mind?"

Are your faculties focused on burdensome bills?
Has your psyche (mind) run back to the fun you experienced last night?

Does your sagacity or better yet mind wonder how you are going to make a relationship work that is beyond humanistic and hominalistic repair?

Ok I know maybe someone's percipience or for the lack of a better word perception is pressing toward what is being prepared at home to partake

Your thoughts may be tied to spousal/parental arguments and upsetting you so much you have been discouraged

Husband drinking
Wife strung out
Test ahead to take

I really don't know, it could be a multiplicity of things but the question I really would love to be entertained is "What's on your mind?"

I am a witness that every time I enter into the Church my mind is not always on Church

Every now and again I need a paradisiacal psychoanalysis

It has become an epidemic that we come to Church as a break from all the madness we left at home, or on the job, or elsewhere

But me thinks I need to tell you, if your mind is somewhere else other than on God, baby it's in the wrong place

Get your mind right

Listen to what Isaiah this bold and courageous prophet said;
Thou wilt keep him in perfect peace, whose mind stayed on thee; because he trusteth in Thee

We can never avoid strife and struggles but we sure can have peace while we have strife and struggles

1st point
There needs to be a constant commercial

I know you probably don't see it but its there!

Watch this He says:
Thou (God) wilt keep him in perfect peace, whose mind is stayed
He could have said thinks-when it comes to mind

He could have said reminisced-when something reminds you

He could have said remembers-something triggers

He could have said ponders-when you daydream

But he says keeps—plural

Now if you give me something and said I am letting you borrow this, common sense says I have to give it back, but if you say you can keep it, it means its mines forever

He says keeps
(Garrison—troops surrounded)

Otherwise I have to keep keeping my mind on Him

It's like this in order to have a constant commercial I have to have something remind me of Him

When I am at home and look at a bill that is greater than my inflow;
It's time for a commercial, but my God shall supply

When I'm in the doctor's office and they offer some troubling news, it's time for a commercial;
I am the God that healeth thee

When I am driving down the road and receive some bad news on the phone, it's time for a commercial;
I am more than a conqueror

When I am working on the job and someone says something out of the way to me, it's time for a commercial break;
I will make your enemies your footstools

When I am sitting in Church and begin to think about something that is unholy, it's time for a commercial break:
An idle mind is the devil's workshop

You do know that keep means to guard, protect

Usually when you tell a friend we need to talk, it heightens the experience and immediately peaks their curiosity, and they reply by saying; what's on your mind?

2nd point you need a divine disposition

Thou wilt keep him in perfect peace whose *MIND!*

Otherwise the mind in one context is our neurological expression; but here mind represents our lifestyle

Ephesians 2:10—for we are his workmanship created in Christ Jesus unto good works

We were created to live Holy

Watch this the word workmanship derives from Greek word poience which derives from poem which is the ancient word of poet;

Which means we are his masterpieces, are you still with me?

God spoke everything into existence

Light—started skipping across backdrop of the night

Water began to run into hands of the earth

Birds gained confidence and spreaded their wings and flew

But when it came to man he stopped and said boys; let us

Otherwise whoever lives according to the masterpiece He has made will have peace

If I could just outright say it like you would understand it; God doesn't want any part-time lovers

If you are to have this peace you must have a divine disposition

The operative is stayed

Stayed yields that we lean on him
(What happens if somebody is leaning on something sturdy versus something shaky?)

That's how we are; if we keep our minds stayed

3rd point we need situational serenity

No matter what comes we need serenity

Serenity is peace of mind

Peace means Shalom in Hebrew

But watch this in Hebrew Perfect means Peace, Peace
Well in the original translation this is how this verse would read

"Thou wilt keep him in peace, peace, peace, whose mind is
stayed on Thee"
I have to learn that whatever state I am in to be content

This is what I want to leave with you;

Isaiah is saying that if you trust in Him, and your
mind—lifestyle is divine, His peace is your peace

Now that's good news

Because he wants us to know that whatever we are going
through the same peace that His son had, will be yours

I don't know about you, but that sounds mighty good

If I can just keep my mind stayed on Him, I will have that
peace

The peace that was displayed when people talked about Jesus

The same peace that was exhibited while he was being
jumped by Roman soldiers

The same peace when his homeboy Judas betrayed

When I was younger in one of my family's home hung a little plaque that said;

God grant me the serenity to accept the things I cannot change, the courage to change the things I can, and the wisdom to know the difference!

I woke up this morning with my mind stayed

Walking and talking
Singing and praying
Aint no harm to keep your mind

"When Struggle Has A Baby"

James 1:2-4

It is imperative to hasten to impute and impress upon the very carriages of your mind that life can seemingly present itself as unfair

It would behoove and become us to come to the vast reality that cataclysmic is the course that many of us have come

Maybe you have not reached that point; but isn't it somewhat troubling to get one thing straightened out to discover four more have surfaced

I must submit to you this day that James is on target when he boldly suggests that troubles will assail us

I almost feel as if James offers as consolation to us that it really does not matter whose family you are in; situations will present themselves

I hate to upset your pretty presuppositions but James is the brother of Jesus; and he says don't worry trouble is coming

I mean how can you open a conversation saying hey brother be happy when struggles presents itself!

I don't know about you but I am somewhat confused as to why James begins by saying to us that just because I am a leader does not exempt me from struggles

I need you to understand that just because you are a pastor, deacon, mission sister, or laity we are not exempt from struggling

I do appreciate how he mentions this struggle though; he says my brethren, as if to say we are in this thing together

I know my geographical location may differ from yours; but brethren

I understand your marquee may read different than my marquee but brethren

I know your way of worship may differ from my way of worship but as long as we meet up in spirit and in truth; my brethren

Count it all joy

Now watch how he sucks us into a sad situation but dresses it up with happy clothes

He says count it joy when trouble comes; struggles arise

Trials do come to make us strong

The word trial means to stretch

To expand; to utilize the elasticity component that resides in us

Trials can mean from within; or those that are inflicted from without

But what rattles me is the introductory word to the subject matter is when!

The very mentioning of the word *when* suggests that it is inevitable, inexcusable, inescapable, and unavoidable and that it will take place

We just need not miscarry what should be
Trials

We must realize we cannot speed up the process

When

Because patience needs to have her perfect work

When the word perfect is used it is not used as being perfect but rather that the trial will not overtake us

Otherwise what we are in; we know we will be over

Divers *(diverse)* temptations *(people and phenomenon)* mean various trials

If I had to paint a picture I would tell you it means that when people that don't mean you no good; don't worry, you'll have the last laugh

Situations that had you worried will now have you winning

Circumstances that made you praying will now have you praising

Watch this: James says you will have the last laugh

It's right there in the text he says it in his introduction; brethren count it all joy

And joy here means to have a good time to laugh

We used to say the same thing that'll make you laugh will make you cry

But James says the same thing that'll make you cry will make you laugh

Otherwise when you are having trouble; don't start crying as if something has happened

Start laughing because you know the outcome

I know it seems hard, but if you expected it then it wouldn't hurt so badly

Come on he says when people lie on you just go ahead and count it all joy
Scandalize your name
Run rumors on you
Stab you in the back
Start mess
Hurt your feelings

Then James teaches us about the word count

Count in this scripture means to command, in Greek it is: Haig-eh-om-ahee

Which simply means it may be hard . . . but command yourself to laugh in the face of the enemy

Force yourself to have joy when it seems all is lost

We are to rejoice knowing that God is testing us

Patience is what will make us a full grown Christian
Evidently some Christians have never really grown up

Patience comes through suffering and testing

You'll grow up when God finishes working patience

Jean Jacques Rousseau
In the mid 1700's said: *"patience is bitter, but its fruit is sweet"*

The fourth verse is a derivative of the word labour

You know what labour means don't you?

When labour is used here it means periodic contractions

Don't allow every trial and every struggle having you wanting
to throw in the towel

If I threw in the towel every time I had a little struggle, I
would have ran out of towels a long time ago

The baby would not be conceived; Joy

What I'm saying here is don't allow the struggles of life to
turn you around!

Keep holding on to the Word of God

Because if you struggle you ought to know the outcome

Count it all joy

I believe those are the sentiments that the song was implying
"This joy that I have the world

A Good Word On A Sad Day

John 14: 1-6

Story begins with Jesus and His disciples

They have been with Jesus in good times and bad times

Many of us are faced with issues and isolated incidents and begin to fret

There is nothing wrong with your heart being hurt; it just means that it should not be troubled

Troubles with our hearts;
Spouse leaving
Child going contrary
Bad decisions
Death

These troubles are not really troubles

Nothing is worse than death

Otherwise we need to trouble our troubles

Which is worse—the actual hypodermic injection in the doctor's office or the anticipation of walking into an office waiting to be worked on and given an explanation of what's wrong?

Don't let your heart shudder

Let not your heart be concerned
Let not your heart flutter
Let not your heart become faint

It may look like the walls are closing in but don't let your hearts

It may seem as if the sides are caving in, but don't let

Not only does he tell us what not to do; but he then tells us what to do

You see because when you trust in God you are trusting in me

Otherwise you've been with me, you know how I am

But when I leave trusting in Him is the same as trusting in me

You see because you cannot go directly through Him without sending your mail to my address

The way to have an untroubled heart is to believe in Him

Contagious yet consoling
Jolly, jovial and smiling
You must be anchored in John 14

Doesn't mean that you will not hurt, it just means that you are not going to let your heart be troubled

You see when you are troubled; you worry

When you are troubled you begin to stress
Pace the floor

Continually question God
Nervous breakdown

Beloved what Jesus is trying to convey or communicate to us
is that the heart which is the muscular organ that pumps blood
and circulates life through our bodies is important

Otherwise if you stop the blood from doing what it does; you
will start having problems all over the body

But when you trust
You can't help but hold your head up high

Listen to the tense he uses

He say ye (you) believe
Not you believed
Not you shall believe

But ye believe in God, believe also in me

Otherwise I believe he is able t do what I need him to do
I believe he can fix it

I believe he will be a company-keeper

I believe he will hold my hand

I believe he will wipe the tears from my eyes

I believe he is who he says he is

Well we know to believe but what do we believe him to do

"In my Father's house are many mansions: if *it were* not so, I would have told you I go to prepare a place for you

<u>Close with "And if I go . . ."</u>

Somebody needs to understand; he said *if* here because he was still here

The Message In The Mud

John 9:6

Some people can only see to the mud, while others see through the mud

Mud is a substance that when smeared on a surface it causes the vision to be impaired

Howbeit that this man's vision was already impaired but Jesus intensifies his impairing

Mud is a substance that is compiled of dirt and water

Dirt is that which is the common denominator for mess

But water is the thing that cleanses and purifies

But together it creates a messier situation

Tis an earthy matter that comes when water kisses the earth

This chapter unfolds by saying that Jesus saw

I just want to real briefly share with you that this man is blind, cannot see at all

But the scripture states that Jesus saw

Jesus sees you when you cannot see yourself

Otherwise when you cannot see your surroundings he can

But after Jesus saw; he went

But watch what the church people do

Master what did he do, or was it his mama'nem?

For it states "I must work the works of him that sent me, while it is day; the night cometh, when no man can work

Two things about this sanctified statement

Secondly it does not say when night cometh, it says that night will come

In other words this man's blindness was timed by God
Jesus told him to go & wash

Notice he didn't promise him he was going to heal him he just said go and wash

Jesus rebukes the disciples without even recognizing

Notice the man never asked any questions he just did it

Because if you have dealt with a thing long enough you will not ask any questions you will just do it

Did you say give them a hundred dollars; ok I will

Did you say bless them with some groceries; ok

Did you say go and pray for them; consider it done

They started murmuring; is that him; some said yeah that's him; others said no it just looks like him

He says: it's me ya'll; I know you don't recognize me because I aint as bad off as you had me, but it's me

Realize that this man has never seen Jesus because he was blind

Look in verse he says 12—"I don't know"

In verse 25 he says "I don't know"

But then he says but this one thing I do know

I went & washed
& now I stand seeing

Look at this he didn't know where Jesus was

He didn't know who Jesus was
But he knew about Jesus
He didn't know Jesus' title
He didn't know how he did it
He didn't know how Jesus looked
But one thing I do know

I may not know how he did it; but I do know he did it

But I got something in me that won't let me hold my peace

Because I can't breakdown how I was healed but I know I was healed

I don't know how the molecular structure took place in the
retinas of my eye
I don't know if he did invisible nerve work
Or if he dilated my pupils

But I do know this

I can hear him saying;
You want to know what I saw alright then:

(He made medicine out of mud)

What appears to be insane to others will be imperative for
some

Nobody sinned this was for my glory

Some others have the same thing; Lazarus he used his
authoritative voice as it penetrated and protruded the
panoramic plight of these sisters

Jesus had been not long evicted by the Gadarean people

I mean who was he; they perhaps had signs around town posted
looking for this man who is supposed to be the son of God

But he doesn't check out; Mary and Joseph are his parents

Fact finders
Discreditors
Nosey people
Finding negatives

What school of ophthalmology did he study at?

He did not examine the lachrymal gland and the iris of his eye

Jesus sees the problem but the problem doesn't see him

He was born this way but he will not die this way

Jesus sees a blind man; observation

Disciples says who sinned; investigation

No one sinned; information

My glory; confirmation

I must work; determination

Sent me; dedication

I am the light of the world; revelation

Mud in his eyes; humiliation

Go wash; participation

Came seeing; restoration

Didn't know who Jesus was; speculation

They begin to talk; communication

Now I see; jubilation

He found out who Jesus was; salvation

The Golden Years

Luke 12: 15-21

There is a peculiar incident happening in the text

Jesus is standing around and there is a man who raises a concern

His concern is that his brother has some money that belongs
to him

Listen to how Jesus responds to this young man

He does not say servant

He does not say child

He simply cuts to the chase and says man

Continue listening to the conversation because Jesus says:
who do I look like to you?

An arbitrator
Lawyer
DA
Judge

The problem was not if the plaintiff or defendant was right; it
is what we do with what we have

In the Apocrypha in the Wisdom of Solomon; the writer speaks of
being messed up behind; when we are nothing but clay ourselves

Otherwise, why are we so engulfed in clay when that's all we are ourselves?

It's like this clay holding clay we are the same it cannot benefit us to be holding onto what we are

He wanted to store up his crops in something bigger because he never disburse of any that he had

It's a shame when we don't want to share anything

Wealth
Money
Concepts
Knowledge
Wisdom
Word
Testimony

This is the only place in the Bible that speaks of retirement

I know that we are well aware of what retirement is all about

Retirement is ok when you have aged, or your physical attributes have been kissed by sickness

But the misconception is thinking that retirement is to bring some things to a squelching halt

The story we are considering this morning suggests that the problem with this man's retirement package was that he wanted everything for himself

For he said let me eat, drink, and be merry

A retirement that lives for self is unbiblical and immoral simultaneously

This man was living as if there were no God

You can plan your retirement to change positions in the sun

You can plan a retirement to meet the needs for your twilight years

You can plan a retirement to plan menus so that the finest cuisines cross your lips

But if you have not helped anybody, your retirement is useless and displeasing to God

You know and since we are in the season of giving me thinks I need to tell you since you have been blessed with much you should be willing to give to somebody else

Notice how Jesus begins this story with super urgency

Take heed,
Beware

It's quite odd to start out saying take heed and then tack on beware

This implies that it's mighty dangerous to be in the company and/or be the person who behaves as such

He uses two words that are somewhat conflicting

I mean the two words he chooses to place in the conversation are disturbing

You do know that in your Golden years are suppose to be your best years

Watch what he does he places the two words I and my loosely in the conversation

He uses I; six times and my five times, but in the Greek he uses I eight times and my six times

But either way it yet implies that he is concerned about one thing

I, me, and my

Whenever you concern yourself about I, me and my, that is who you'll end up spending most of your time with

Watch this, that's why he said I'll say to my soul

Why would you want to spend your last years as being your loneliest years?

I know it's somewhat abrupt but the last years are your golden years

Watch this; everything is better with age

Wine is better aged; I know what you're thinking

What did the officials say in Cana?

You saved the best for last

Anniversaries are symbolized as silver 25 Years

Golden at 50 years

Watch what happens to this man in his foolish state

God was so displeased he said *Thou* fool tonight your soul is required of thee

Notice how God grants his request without him even knowing that he had a request

He said your soul

That was his problem the whole while; he never gave his life nor his soul to Christ

I used to wonder why he called this man a fool

I know now, it was because this man was claiming something that did not belong to him

You should never retire for working for the Lord

Noah was 500 when God instructed him to build the ark

In Luke Anna was eighty-four years of age and the scripture said she didn't depart from the temple

Abraham was 100 and Sarah was 90 they kept working for God

Caleb at eighty-five when he fought for the Lord

That's why I say to you again my brothers and sisters don't let time steal your task

I believe that's why they would open their prayers and say I thank you for letting my golden moments roll on a little while longer

Remember these are the "Golden Years"

Worship In The Water

Matthew 14:27

We have heard this preached many times throughout our lives

Some would speak about storms; there are always storms in our lives

Others would speak about get out of the boat; there are instances whereas the normal is not the needed

Then there are even those who spoke about water walkers; being the person that would have faith enough to do the impossible; walk on water!

But evidently in this text this morning, god revealed a new thing to me; worship in the water

After all there is a storm in the text

Yes, after all there is the necessity to get out of the boat

There is the reality of having enough faith to do the impossible

But we cannot overlook how to worship in the water!

Jesus constrained them; THEN . . . He went on His away . . . the scripture says . . . up into the mountains

How did He go away on water . . . because . . . He went into the mountains, and the only way to get to the mountains was on water . . .

Now my question was why did he go up ON a mountain . . . I'll tell you why Jesus went UP ON a mountain . . .

It's because in the physical Jesus wanted to see their reaction to the storm . . .

Front row seats . . .

If you can't get it on the shore . . . he will test you on the sea . . .

The Holy Writ says whilst they were in the midst of the sea . . . a storm arose . . .

Watch this: the ship was in the midst of the sea . . . the storm arose IN the sea not on the sea . . .

The problem was not the water it was the chaos in the water . . .

You are missing this . . . your problem aint with nobody its chaos within that person . . .

Listen to what Jesus says . . .

Jesus came walking on the water . . .

He came walking ON what they were IN . . .

Be of Good cheer . . . cheerleaders cheer whether it's good or bad . . . but their cheer (nature) is dependent upon the situation . . . give example!!!

But here it says . . . use a good cheer even in a bad situation . . . as if you are winning . . .

Jesus comes walking on what had them scared . . .

Walking on the sea in Greek-PAH-THE-OH . . . meaning . . . trample . . .

In order to trample you need many feet . . . after thanksgiving sale . . . black Friday . . .

People die from being trampled on . . . things are crushed in trampling . . .

Something heavy flattens what's has us delirious . . .

Well, what was He trampling on . . . simple the sea . . . what was in the sea . . . the problems that had them frightened . . .

What was in the sea . . . chaos . . . ?

Jesus came walking on what was in the sea . . . why to trample and flatten it out . . .

What was Jesus really doing . . . walking it out . . . ?

I could shout right now . . .

Listen to the mentioning of sea . . .

Now after Jesus comes walking they were troubled as the Bible says . . .

But did you hear what Jesus says while they are troubled . . . while they are in a storm . . .

Be of good cheer . . .

Let me hope you out and this ought to shout you . . .
Be of good cheer . . . means SHOUT RIGHT NOW . . .

Right where you are scared
Agitated
Troubled
Frustrated

Shout right there . . .

He said shout first . . .
Look next . . .

I thought you were with me . . . Get happy now . . . then says
"It is I"

Otherwise, get this . . . shout before you see me . . . better
yet . . . shout before you know it is me . . .

Then focus in on Peter he says: "Lord if it's you . . ."
Fractured Friendship
Messed up Marriage
Sometimey Sister
Backbiting brother
Jacked up Job
Chattering Church member

IT IS I . . .

Greek it is I-I AM WHAT I WILL BE . . .

Notice what Peter asked . . . bid me to walk on what has me
frightened and confused

Man Up

I Corinthians 13:11

Have you ever known a man that appears to be a man, walks like a man, sounds like a man, even acts like a man?

But in essence his mentality does not line up with his masculinity . . .

I was profoundly perturbed at the presentation of most men these days

Because it used to be if you looked like a man you were a man . . .

Carl Gustav Jung wrote in one of his publications: it is not starvation, not microbes, not cancer, but man himself who is mankind's greatest danger . . .

I think I ought to tell you the young people used to have a saying whenever something were about to jump off or something was about to go down . . .

They would gear themselves up to handle the situation . . .

If there was a male there that seemed as if he was cowardice; they would simply say man up . . .

I mean if you going to be grown; you might as well act the part . . .

I found out that Paul was speaking to men who have the wrong mentality about being men . . .

Just because you can woo a woman does not qualify you as being a man . . .

Just because you have money in the bank and some to spare; does not make you a man . . .

1st point
In order to Man up you have to speak up

Philippians 3:20:
For our conversation is in Heaven; from whence we also look for our Saviour, the Lord Jesus Christ

Watch this when a child is born and first begins to speak what do you hear?
Goo-goo
Gaa-gaa

The only reason the baby says Goo-goo and Gaa-gaa; is because they just put whatever they can together to try and be like everybody else . . .

Otherwise it's like this: there ought to come a time in every man's life that you are no longer talking about things that make no sense at all . . .

You ought to raise your conversation . . .

I mean how is it you are 45 years old and still only have to talk about what you used to do; you need to be talking about things right now . . .

I didn't mean to go this hard but let me drop this whilst I'm
already there . . .
Why is that most men upon coming to church know about the
bible but cannot find anything in the Bible . . .
Raise your conversation . . .
(Only repeating what everybody else has said . . .)

The b part of this scripture is whatever a child says; is a direct
witness of who he is been around . . .
(If you speak Spanish the child will speak Spanish)

Many men cannot talk about the word because they are not
around the Word . . .

2ⁿᵈ point
In order to Man up you have think up

Philippians 4:8:
Finally brethren, whatsoever things [are] true, whatsoever things
[are] honest, whatsoever things [are] just, whatsoever things
[are] pure, whatsoever things [are] of good report; if [there be]
any virtue, and if [there be] any praise, think on these things

Beloved what Paul says here is imperative; because he says;
when I was a child I spake as a child and I understood as a
child . . .

I'm not going to stay here long but let me incite you here . . .
Otherwise I use to reason as a child . . .

My thought patterns were of a child . . .

One of the things I use to do as a child was; I thought
everything was funny . . .

I use to play about everything . . .

But Paul says here I elevated my thinking to another level . . .

Whereas when I was younger I expected less; now that I am older I expect more . . .

I see this one's going to be hard . . .
Ok, if I am going to think higher I have to focus on something bigger than me . . .

The bible says I'll keep you in perfect peace whose mind is stayed on me . . .

I wish somebody in here would just holler man up . . .

3rd point
In order to Man up you have to grow up

I know someone is going to be angry at this last point . . .
So a man thinketh in his heart so is he?

Some men are too attached to their childhood . . .

Babies when they are small would need to be changed but stayed in their mess until somebody changed them . . .

I know it's hard but it's on time . . .

Men we need to grow up so that our homes are right . . .

Communities
Churches
World

We allow the world to steal our children . . .
Man up . . .

We allow the world to steal our little boys and grow up liking
other little boys . . .
Man up . . .

We allow the world to steal our little girls to grow up and not
expect anything from a man but to lie with him, because that's
all they see their father's doing . . .
Man up . . .

We allow the world to divide our families through finance . . .
Man up . . .

We allow the world to come in and steal our praise on Sunday
morning; because it's not manly to praise the Lord . . .
Man up . . .

Somebody else ought to say I'm not just going to look the
part; I am going to be the part . . .

If you know that it has been nobody but the Lord who brought
you over shake somebody's hand, give them dap and say real
men praise the Lord . . .

If he kept you from all hurt, harm, and danger, tell somebody
you need to go ahead and man up . . .

When I was a child . . .
I acted like a child . . .
Walked like a child . . .
Behaved like a child . . .
Cried at all the wrong times . . .
Broke valuable things . . .

I went places I didn't have business going . . .

But when I became a man . . .

I didn't forget what it was to be a child . . .
I didn't forget about what I did as a child . . .
I didn't forget about life as a child . . .

But I did put them away . . .

That's what we need to do is put them away . . .

Preaching On E

I Corinthians 9: 13, 14

There is an evolutionary epidemic that is rapidly ransacking the oppositional outlook on Pastor's and preachers these days

There is a definite disconnect in the discourse from the people to the preacher

I am certain and positive that this must be cleared up

I believe Paul with a hint of subtlety secretly shares with us that the problem is camouflaged in the facade that should rest in our character

I believe that we should be aware that there is a misconception In our pews concerning the pulpit

But we must come to grips that there is a missing link in the chain of progress in the Church

I have been driving now for 20 plus years now and I have yet to see a vehicle travel far and efficiently without any fuel

I am almost sure that if I were to leave from Longview on my way to Dallas; if my gas hand is on E but my destination requires it to be on F, then we have a problem

I don't intend to walk softly this afternoon!

I really don't know how far to go with this

Paul announces something from the annals of eternity that we must not acquire situational amnesia

Listen ever so intently; Paul says "Even so hath the Lord ordained that they which preach . . ."

I struggled with this text something vigorously

It drained me to get an answer out of the text of what the exegetical enlightenment was to explain

Now this word *of* kind of squirmed its way into my message

Yes this finite and fickly preposition politely places itself in this preachment

The preposition of suggests that it expresses a relationship between the object—gospel and the subject which is preachment

This two-letter word almost leaps up and screams talk about me

Ok *of* what do you want to talk about?

Well in order to tell you what I do mean; I need to first tell you what I do not mean

If I had of been replaced with the word by, it would weaken the scripture

Because by says the word may work or it may not work

God does not want the preacher's welfare to be predicated upon suggesting an iffy Gospel

If I had of been replaced with through, there would be a waiting period

So he uses me to say; *of* the Gospel, so whether or not you see it, it will happen, so take care of the man of God and you will see results

A wise man once said:
Scandalous maintenance breeds scandalous ministers and ministries

Preaching ought not to be something that he is diverted from, nor disturbed in it

You see the problem here was the Corinthian church recognized the rights of others to receive support but had tragically neglected Paul
(3 year Anniversary—and he said I suffered all things, hunger, deprivations and did so silently, he told no one because someone would have charged him with being worldly minded or in it for money)

Let me share with you what ought to be done

The priests of old were supported by the tithes of the crops Number 18:21, 24

What happened was that the priests at first received a stipend of the offerings at Lord's Supper

Then at love feast according to his ability, when the table was taken care of, the bishop laid aside a portion for himself, and the rest went to widows, orphans, and the poor

Now the Levites

(Assistant ministers, armor bearers—because they shielded the priest from judgment of people)

Were to receive as well; they were to assist the priests, to keep guard, temple was clean, prepare supplies for sanctuary, oil, wine, incense

Not off of sacrifices but from first fruits

Meat offering—what was set aside for holy unto God?

Wave offering—for the preacher's entire family
First fruit offering—finest of the harvest which meant that God and the priest received the better of the first

Living of the gospel means: when the word accomplishes that which we promulgate that you ought to reciprocate

It's like this when you are blessed you ought to bless the man of God

He also says if I wanted to be married and have a family it would be yours to take care of my family

Paul says I should not have to have a side job either

Well brother preacher what is preaching?

The primacy of preaching is to help somebody see Jesus in their predicament

Preaching is waking up at midnight to a call that someone in the church has crossed over

Preaching is when a marriage that was about to give out spoke with the preacher and now they are hanging in there

Preaching is when your mind is in a fix and you need a regulator
Preaching the transliterated word is Kerygma a Greek noun meaning a message or proclamation
(9 times in New Testament)

Kerygma means to preach fervently

It means to give of yourself
It means to empty one's self

Fervent means to put your whole being into it

Kerygma is to offer the doctrine
(What is right?)

Kerygma is to offer Reproof
(What is wrong?)

Kerygma is to offer Correction
(How to get right)

Kerygma is to offer Instruction in righteousness
(How to stay right)

Preaching is telling the truth

What is going on now days is not really preaching

Its motivational speaking

When you speak a feel good message preaching has not been presented

Kerygma is contextualizing—to make it applicable to whoever the audience is

Many pulpits are lacking the preaching that is needed

Let me ease on down the road

You know when you are on empty your car starts sucking up trash and everything and can mess up
(Scripture that says that he stand with joy)

The message is not empty but many times the messenger is empty

You know it's sad:
That we put gas in a car tank that transports us from point a to point b, but will not put gas in a man that can direct us from earth to glory

We end up using our energy and everything having to work

Car starts puttering:
We can get out of the car all that is capable of doing so we get every other thrust

Starts hesitating:
It almost thinks about doing what it knows it is built to do, but now because it does not have the fuel . . .

All I Want For Christmas

Matthew 6:33

We are right in the heart of the Christmas season and
practically everyone is looking for something

Some people want a new car

Others are expecting a tennis bracelet, or a ring

While some anxiously await the big question to be popped

Younger ones are filled with anxiety looking for an iPod
touch or a new game system

When some are expecting the simple things in life such as a
warm and hot meal

Believe it or not there are those who simply would like to
have a place to lay their head for an hour or two

But the fact of the matter is; our priorities are mixed up

Verse 32 implies that he knows what we need
(He knows what we need and what we want)

He speaks to us by the way and says you are looking for
many things but the one thing you use as a back-up should be
your first resort

Seek means to worship zeteo in Greek
(Zah-tay-o)

Go after, strive, pursue

Require—can't function without it
(Batteries required)

I know it looks good
I know you want it

But if there are no batteries it won't work

Seek after Him and then seek for others to become a part of
the kingdom

But more times than not our misinterpretation is in numerical
order and we have forgotten about chronological order kissed
by logikos order

Otherwise we try to put physical things before spiritual things
and it slips our minds that Spiritual time was here before
physical time ever existed

So that tells me before there was ante meridiem and post
meridiem/ am and pm there was God

Before there ever was time, God was time

The cause for worry is seeking after worldly things

Worldly things can only taste good, feel good, and look good

But they cannot touch the inside of man

You cannot satisfy your inward man with outward
attachments

1st point-Anything broken ought to be fixed
I mean why would the Lord start a sentence of with but

But is a conjunction that cancels out the previous statement

Implies there needs to be a change

You know usually when someone says but, it indicates that
what you said or tried didn't work

Seek, find and follow

2nd point-
He says our reward for not seeking things is to receive things
(Children—they'll ask for something and then you say no,
because you haven't been doing what I ask you to do, but
when they do it you are reminded what they wanted and they
are rewarded)

II Chronicles 1:11, 12

The prodigal son

3rd point-
There is an unto clause

I'll do for you until you mess up

Deal with contrasts between until and unto

Until is conditionally

Until says I'll continue until you get on my nerves

Upset me

Cross me
Frustrate me

Watch what Jesus says before unto, this is the shouting piece
Added

Added—lay beside, give more, and increase

When the writer says added he uses a strategic word to infer
that when you add something it is only to better what it is you
are creating

In making a cake the recipe says add an egg because if the
egg is not added the cake will fall and become flat

In working upon receiving a raise they have to add more
money to get a greater figure

In marriage you add a male and a female to become one
couple

If it wasn't for adding everything would be bland and dull

But one thing needs no adding, that is the word of God;

He says don't add and don't take away

Well preacher what are you telling me?

Ok let me say it like this if you need anything to remain, you
ought to let God do the adding

Because when God does the adding the adding, this ought to
bless you

When God does the adding, his adding is better than ours

Because when we add sometimes it subtracts from us

When we add it divides us

But when God adds, it multiplies

Watch this, when David walked through the valley, he had the opportunity to sit down, and he said my cup runneth over

When Dr Luke tells us Christ said he yields to us;

Give and it shall be given unto you, good measure, pressed down;

Otherwise it won't fit but I will make it fit

Then he said running over

I tell you God's adding is better than ours

The multitude on the mountainside hungry but no food . . .

I wish you tell about two or three people let God do the adding it just works out better

Go and hug four people and tell them All I want for Christmas is God, if I get him I'll receive what I been searching for

Tell'em I might want something else but He is number one

Darkness Falls

Luke 23:44

And it was about the sixth hour, and there was darkness over all the earth until the ninth hour

My dear brothers and sisters what we have here is an account of Jesus' darkest day

I've heard many scientists and intellectual inspired fellows testify to the fact that;

Socrates was such a good man
I've heard that MLK was a great leader
It has been stated that Apollo's was a great orator
But if they have decreed that Socrates lived and died like a philosopher
MLK lived and died like a leader
Apollo's lived and died like a great orator
Then Jesus lived and died like a God

What I see leaping from this page of the Law of Liberty is that we will all encounter some dark days

So I stand this night to help us understand the significance in the darkness

We will all encompass some stormy and stirring days

As a matter of fact I would be so bold to share with you problems will come

They are inevitable
They are inescapable
They are inexcusable

You cannot get away from dark days

In this life we are going to have to answer some cataclysmic calls

We will become entangled in a few catastrophic happenings

Darkness is a very confusing state

I mean after all if we were to but turn out the lights right now and try to escape it would be very difficult
(Turn out the lights)

Notice the scripture says from the sixth to the ninth hour which is 12:00 pm it was dark

The time whereas you would have lunch

The time by which we take a break from hard work, the sixth hour that is

The part of the day where the Sun is the hottest

The slot in nature's time clock where the sun puts in most work
The sixth hour

I'm trying to help you but you aint . . .

At twelve noon it should be the brightest part of the day, but now it's the darkest

I think a commercial would suffice here sometimes in life when it should be the most happiest time of your life it will turn out to be the most darkest time of your life

You see what happened was the sun was eclipsed and the air exceedingly clouded at the same time, both which caused to this thick darkness to fall,

Otherwise what was happy was blocked by something sad and stood in front of that happy thing and clouded it with a somber substance to cause the darkness

It must have been a great day when God stood above the elliptic of the earth and cried out "Let there be light" and light came and laid down on the hammock of the night

It must have been a great day when God bent over that lump of clay and dirt started discharging air

It must have been a great day when God flung with his flaming fingers the stars, and set them in orbits throughout the universe

It must have been a great day when he raised mountains as little children, and pointed and coursed the rivers and seas

It had to be a great day when John the Baptist was able to sing Take me to the water and realized he was baptizing the Water in some water

It must have been a great day when Jesus suspended nature and physics and made a waterway into a walkway

It must have been a great day when Jesus came to Lazarus' grave and told death stop fooling yourself, loose him and let him go

Those were some great days, but the greatest happened right here on this skull shaped hill

Beloved in spite of this being a great day you cannot help but see these mean, maniacal, messed up mentalities of his accusers

If you really want to see the blackness of mankind's heart come here to Calvary

There was so much wickedness poured upon Christ here at Golgotha

From 9:00 until 12:00, Christ hangs here openly before men

During these 1st three hours 9:00 am until 12:00 pm men curse him, antagonize him, and ridicule him

But then the earth quakes, the rocks break, the wind blows, and the darkness comes

Now from 12 until 3, there is the darkness of hell

The sun was confused and covered its eyes as it had not witnessed this happen to its creator before to be handled so unfairly

The Heavens were astonished and horribly afraid and withdrew themselves

I mean it was light that gave intelligence to the birth of Jesus why not be ushered out by darkness

This is why I need to tell you darkness does fall

When darkness fell on the land, his final words were spoken

As a matter of fact when darkness fell nature responded

If you don't believe me the bible whispers at that moment nature took up being a seamstress and cut the curtain in the temple in twain

This allows us intimate access to God?

When darkness fell on the earth nature responded with an earthquake, it says the earth shook

When darkness fell it says the rocks could not contain themselves

Darkness ran by the graves of the holy ones who were sleeping in the confines of their graves and set off the alarm to awaken them and witness the grand event

Beloved when darkness fell, the city would never be the same

Too much has happened

I mean earthquakes taking place, shattering rocks, cemetery resurrections, this wasn't an ordinary day

I imagine the chief priests and high priests couldn't sleep due to the transpirings

I mean I can hear Pilate's wife creeping up to his ear in anguish saying; I told you to leave him alone

Can you see Mary, Jesus mother having hope breathed into her heart?

This was extraordinary darkness

I wondered and I pondered when we speak about this darkness that turned the lights out

Could it be satan who turned them out?

Naw, because if Jesus is the light of the world and satan hit the switch his light would shine

I came to the conclusion that the only one with ultimate power was God

Psalms 22:3 says God is a holy God, and he could not stand to look at sin which Jesus was carrying

That's how it is from time to time in all of our lives

The Lord desires to elevate us but he has to turn the lights out

Look at somebody and says he has to turn out the lights sometimes

He has to turn out the lights in order for us to powerfully proclaim that it was God . . .

1st point when darkness falls
There is a struggle
Ephesians 6:12
For we wrestle not against
Paul says there is a struggle

Listen whenever you allude to speaking about darkness, you cannot associate darkness with God

He has no place IN darkness but to accentuate it
(John 1:5)

Jesus was wrestling with the powers of darkness

Listen when we have issues in life don't worry because we know they will come

Secondly if we have Jesus we have a light in us that the enemy cannot understand

2ⁿᵈ point
When darkness falls
It becomes a setup
(Psalms 30:5)

We now see Jesus fight them on their own turf

He allows the darkness to reign for a little while

God suspends the light from the sun

You find that Jesus allows them to think they have him just where they want him

Jesus has died and they see him no longer being a threat

But they have not yet felt the tremors in the ground yet

They have not yet heard the doors to the caskets creeping open

They have not heard the rocks yawning from their sleep

They have not felt the wind play tag from here and yonder

It was a setup
In all of our lives know this when enemies think they have
you right where they want you tell them read the small print

Look at somebody else and say you should have read the
whole thing

Luke 22::53
When I was daily with you in the temple, ye stretched forth
no hands against me; but this is your hour, and the power of
darkness

Because what they don't see is Jesus said it they just didn't listen

I hear the songwriter singing what the devil meant for bad,
God turned it for my good

I love how Yolanda Adams says it though in the battle is not
yours;

God is just setting you up for a blessing

3rd point
When darkness falls h*ell is confused*

This particular account says it was the sixth hour and
darkness fell until

Well brother preacher was does that mean?
I'm glad you asked

It means satan had his time even with our Lord but it was only until

I wish I could help you understand

What I'm saying here is your trials, your troubles; your tribulations are only until

But when God got ready to diminish the darkness he did

I just wish somebody would know that although it may be little dark right now, it only until

He won't put on you more . . .

Dinner Time

Psalms 23:5

I am inclined to believe that many have concluded that this verse is one that should be savored and saved for saints that now sleep with our Saviour

But I would have you know that this particular passage is to remind us that there is revitalization, rejuvenation, and refreshing in coming to the table . . .

You see David silently slips in a swift swing to the sweet scripture when it transitions us from walking in a valley to sitting at a table . . .

There is good news tucked away in this verse

Because in life I am a witness of some valley experiences . . .

Yeah I can testify to having walked through some trying times

I can submit a deposition that I have been so low I couldn't see up, but thank God there was more to the story

What David was attempting to convey to us is that sometimes it takes you to slow down in order to see He was there all the time

He was saying He prepared; He took time and made *arrangements* for me

Watch this;

Prepared means he slowed down enough to set up, think about, and plan for my arrival

I really don't know how to chew it up any more to dress your plate with it

Otherwise this wasn't thrown together

This was no fluke
This is not happenstance
This is not leftovers I'm trying to get rid of; I took time and worked to get this prepared for you

I can almost hear God saying I slaved in my heavenly home to get this ready

What God had waiting on me; get this; gives life, because I just finished walking through the valley?

Listen I just experienced being threatened by death

I just finished almost dying on the operating table
Losing my job
Losing my marriage
Home being foreclosed on
Evicted from apartment
Car being repoed

But he took out time that when I came out a table was spread

He says I have:
Table spread
Cup filled
Meat for his hunger

And all you have to do is sit down and partake of what I have for you
Watch this, the table and oil is not just a onetime thing he does this daily

EST on the end of prepares means to repeat process

But watch this it further describes the word described

It serves as a suffix that is a superlative degree of an adjectives and/or adverbs

Adjectives are describing words, adverbs are used as modifiers

So what he does he uses a suffix that is magnified to what we expect, but less than he speaks of

Otherwise He uses the greatest of words in our vocabulary to explain what we can expect in front of our enemies

It's like this I want you to know that what I have for you is greater than what you expect

Enemies also mean pains here

If a soldier eats in the presence of enemies he eats quickly to return to battle

Nothing is hurried

The enemy has been given notice

He had protection for as long as he stayed there

The hosts were expected and required to protect their guests at all costs
So if I am in your house my life is not just in my hands it is in your hands now

They were protected and after they ate and rested by a stone wall that surrounded them

And the shepherd would sleep across the entrance of the doorway

He would become the door

Otherwise if you want to get to them you have to go through Him

You know how it was when you got to where your big brother or big sister or daddy you would lick your tongue out or say you can't get me, only because if you could make it to them you were protected

Then He says thou anointest my head with oil

The oil in near eastern culture at a banquet it was customary to anoint with fragrant oil

So it doesn't matter what it may smell like he has fragrance for your situation

The oil was refreshing and soothing

The shepherd had to study the nature of the grass, poisonous plants, reptiles, preying animals

Noticing the condition of the sheep as they come in

Using the oil to anoint scrapes, wounds, scratches, bruises

The oils would be applied to head and horns to keep flies and other insects

Otherwise things that were nagging

You do know some things can become irritating in life

Not only can some things but some people can become irritating and instead of taking a swing at them

He anoints your head with oil

You do know that sheep could swat like we swat so he would massage the oil in
In other words God would put something on us that serves as a repellent

I see you still aren't getting this; he places on and in us something that keeps them from bothering us
Some of us need some off

You remember the other day he said resist the devil that's the repellent and he will flee from you

Listen to how David concludes this meal date

He says my cup runneth over as if to say I cannot contain myself

But then there is another twist to the implication David has given us

My cup runneth over, I have not only enough for me but my friends to

If you stick with me you can be blessed off my overflow

If you sit close enough to me my cup will overflow

If you keep talking to me my cup will run over

And when my cup overflows guess what you will be able to receive what I receive

In the message bible it says you give me a six course dinner right in front of my enemies

Contemporary English version says you treat me to a feast while my enemies watch

I think I need to tell you the table is worship; translation is something to place the food upon

He prepares personal provisions

Thou preparest a table before *me* in the presence of *mine* enemies

Otherwise you fix for me what I like while my own enemies watch me
Other people are at the table but I have what I desire

That's how we can say:
What God has for me

Friends

Mark 2:1-6

Years ago there was a song put out about this very subject, some of you may be too saved to remember it

But the songs go as such: Friends, how many of us have them Friends, one's we can depend on

Which undoubtedly shares with us a friend should be dependable

A friend should be a shoulder to lean on

A friend should be one that does not have to be asked to assist you he/she is one that senses your need before it is ever expressed

You see a true friend will carry your burdens when it seems unbearable for you

They are one that should be able to encourage when you are discouraged

I did say a friend didn't I

But the sad truth that plagues us today is that friends in these days and times are fickled
They are more hidden than those you don't even know

I heard a former Deacon Kenton Kelly of a Church I Preached at say: one day that caller id has ruined our world

I hold that for being the truth

Because a friend will not look at the display on the caller id and see your name and ignore it as if you had never called

I mean a true friend will answer the call with altruism (unselfishness) and anticipation

Listen if you have to wonder whether or not someone is your friend then truth be told they are not

I wanted to examine this eschatological embodiment of efforts

Look into the text and you would find a story that shares an idea of friendship

It is the very show of what and how friends should be
Firstly take notice to the fact that the interpolation or introduction in this passage says that Jesus is the attraction

I think I would less than a preacher I would less than a mail carrier if I didn't tell you something

If Jesus is not the centralized calling and becomes centrifugal in calamities then it's really not a friendship

Otherwise if your friendship is built around anything other than Christ it cannot be categorized as a friendship

But look Mark says it was noised that Jesus was in the house

I am poignantly persuaded that I should park for a moment

I would like to give a few indicators of friends and foes

If a person would rather take you partying than churching they are not . . .

If they would rather get you high than slain in the spirit . . .

They would rather keep the money you overpaid you than pay it back

Encourage you to do wrong thing rather than do right thing

Help you talk about somebody than correct your conversation

Take you to a Teddy Pendergrass or Usher concert than go to hear your Pastor preach

Then you know they are not a friend

Scriptures says and holds to the point that when they heard that Jesus was in revival, on a preaching platform they took their friend

When they heard about the revival they took

Listen took is a possessive word, and is topped off with an imperative meaning

The word took indicates that it was of importance to get him in the state that he was in to where Jesus was

I'm glad they didn't have the same mindset that we have

Well whenever you get ready to start living differently, healed, delivered we'll be here for you

They simply said in deeds the time is now

They will say to me the time is now

No more drinking
No more smoking
No more slipping and tipping
No more cheating
No more

The time is now

Tell somebody the time is now

Friends need to push you to where you need to be
I'm not saying they can save you but they can get you where
salvation is

They cannot baptize you but they can get you to where public
confession can take place

They cannot wash you whiter than snow but they can get you
to where cleansing takes place

They cannot change you but they can take you to where
change is

Friends will take you where the one is that can make a
difference

Let me pause here parenthetically and tell you everybody that
brings somebody to church; and are here at church; are not
there for the right reason

Some of these people came for cures

But there was some who came out of curiosity
But then others came for church

Mark says there were so many people there wasn't any room
in the doorway to peek over to see in

This means that people where standing up

We all know that when you stand up and others are sitting
down, you can see everything that is going on

But as Jesus was preaching they came up with a plan to get
their friend to Jesus

The bible says they bore him to where Jesus was

That's why it's easy to say friends ought to bear their friends
burden
Scripture says bear one another burdens

When you cannot carry your own, a friend will yield
assistance

Because friends will take you to where progress is

Record holds that they went to the rooftop

Just by them being on the rooftop symbolizes despair

It symbolizes frustration and running out of options

They begin to tear up the roof

Let me show you something

If a man or woman is really your friend then finance will not shy them away

If you need a little help a friend will come through for you

If you need a lot of help they ought to be right along there with you

The bible says they tore up the roof

Shingle by shingle
Tearing up the roof

Digging and scraping tearing up the roof

Removing reed and dirt
Tearing up the roof

Mud and branches
Tearing up the roof

Pulling and tearing destroying the roof

They begin to see light

I wish you could see it like I see it

Otherwise they didn't care how they got him there they just wanted to get him where Jesus was

A friend doesn't care how much; they just want healing

They don't care how long the doctor's wait is they want a good report

They don't care how much you owe them because they are not looking for it in repay
Listen they destroyed the roof, the scripture does not say that they repaid it

Neither does the scripture say they left a deposit

It does not say that they asked how much it will cost to put him through the roof

They just commenced to start tearing up the roof

Oh how awesome it would be to have friends like these

Friends my God that do not even care about the limelight

They never stated the names of these four men

You see because friends don't care about a pat on the back

Friends don't care about their names on your life policy

Friends don't care about you acknowledging them as your friend

Friends really are not concerned about their name; all they want is to get you to Jesus

Beloved I want you to see here that friends will have faith in you when your faith has diminished

Friends will believe in your healing when you have thrown in the towel

I think right now you ought to tell somebody thank God for friends

Listen as the rope or the lowering device is allowing him to be put in the very presence of Christ

Jesus stops what he is doing to heal this man

He says to him because of their faith

He did not see them scripture he says he saw their faith
You did not get it

He does not see the turmoil on the rooftop, he saw their faith

He does not focus on the house now being a mess, he saw their faith

He did not bring up the fact that service has been interrupted, he sees their faith

Well let me move on since you didn't say anything

Whenever you are going though God does not see your situation he sees your faith

If you have faith as a grain . . .

Faith and seeing does not jive with each other

Because he told us the other day that Now Faith is the substance of things hoped for the evidence of things not seen

So if you can see it it's not faith

71

That's good news there

In other words because they are hooked up to me I have to heal your body

I can imagine Jesus saying to him you better thank my father for blessing you with saved friends

Is there anybody here who is glad about saved friends?

Friends how many of us have them

Friends one's we can depend on

But I am so glad I've got a friend in Jesus

But that's not all I want to share with you

There's not a friend like the lowly Jesus, No not one, no not one

Jesus knows all about our problems he will die till the day is done

There's not a fiend like Jesus

This is the one I love

What a friend we have in Jesus all our sins and grief's to bear, what a privilege it is to carry everything

Tell somebody I got a friend I can tell everything

I have a fiend that will not gossip my business

I have a fiend that will not spread rumors on me

I have a friend that love's me dear

I can take everything to God in Prayer

As a matter of fact this friend sticks closer than a brother

This friend dries my eyes
Calm my fears
Walks with me
Comforts me
Speaks to me
Hold m's me
Caresses me
He's my all and all

Tell somebody he's my friend go to about three people and tell he's my friend

Tell somebody you may not see the healing but it's there

Leave The Light On

Matthew 5:16

Motel 6 chain uses as a slogan and Tom Bodett says: "We'll leave the light on for you"

In other words the light will be left on because the light makes you feel welcome

The light creates a sense of comfortability and safety

The light has a sense of direction and directs you to where rest is

I believe in this spiritual stroll through the vehicle of life there ought to be a difference between the world and the church

Call me crazy for addressing the issue at hand but why is it that hardly anyone can differentiate between the saved and the unsaved

I mean there ought to be an office of ostentation in our walk with God

In other words we need to be different

This scripture reeks with the indication of being real but relevant

You know there was a time when you could almost look at someone and tell if they were saved

I mean he does say that men might see . . .

After all the word declares in this job description that we ought to be flavor to the world

But I find more often that the world has become the flavor so to speak, and we have become the taste-testers

We have become so sucked into the world; the world now dictates to us what they want

But I hear God saying through the blow horn of the bible—*Let your light so shine*

As if to say I'm not worried about anybody else I am concerned about you

I know that many times in life we will find ourselves in predicaments that are not of a Christian

But we have to learn how to shine anyhow

This 16th verse is so important that it is Jesus who has now repeated himself

Notice in verse 13 he says you are the salt of the earth

Which makes the two verses synonymous or one in the same

You see a Christian's life should be exemplary (Transparent)

It should be one of influence

The question that arises in this text is anyone intrigued by your light

I wish you would hear what I am saying

Has there been a change in someone else's life based upon yours

Otherwise has your life impacted someone enough to get them saved?

If you aint drawing nobody to Christ something's wrong

The writer says let your light shine

Now pay close attention to this: He likens our lives with a light bulb

Do you know what light bulb does?

The bulb does three things

First and foremost the bulb is made to give light

I think before I move on I ought tell you that we were created to show someone the way

I think that's why the quartet sings that song "Show me the Way"

Now if we are suppose to give light, how can we give light in darkness when our light does not shine?

I mean if we are at the same clubs with the unsaved how can we lead them somewhere we aint

How can we shine when we hitting off the same joint that the lost is?

I don't know about you but if you hooked on pornography and won't let go, how can you shine

I mean if you running into a wino and buying the same beverage at the same store, how is it? That your light can shine

Tell somebody they're watching you

They're watching you when you sleep

Watching you when you work
Watching you as you walk
Listening to you as your speak

They are watching you

So the 1st action of a bulb is it gives off light

Secondly it supplies warmth

In other words people ought to feel warmed by our sense of welcome

If the hurt, helpless, and the harmed don't feel a sense of welcome from you, then is no light in you

I know, if people around you feel uneasy and cannot talk to you then something is not warm It's luke-warm

If I am hurt and can't feel a sense of healing in your being here, you are lacking

Listen I have to be warm to send off a feeling of safety

I have to give off some energy to bring the cold-hearted on in

There are some people that have some cold hearts and only the warmth can melt them down

Otherwise they may hate church but they sure don't mind being in your company

That's because while you are talking they're melting

While you are walking upright before them they are seeing the light from your hot bulb

They see a light at the end of their tunnel because you possess a welcoming spirit

Tell them yes I am; because I have a lamp that puts off energy

I wondered why is it that Jesus uses a little small light bulb to describe his carriers

It came to me that it makes sense to make us lights if he is light of the world

So we know now that the bulb—gives light, and gives warmth

Lastly the bulb burns on the inside but shines on the outside

Somebody is going to catch this on the way home

Burns on the inside but shines on the outside

On the inside of a bulb is a filament that burns slowly but it makes the glass glow

It is the filament that burns up with heat but on the other side of the mirrored glass it shines

What I am trying to say is that God has so fixed us to have a filament which is our soul to burn on the inside but has our countenance to shine on the outside

Let's see, ok I mean when hell has broken lose in our life, and has even affected your neighbor, you'll burn up inside

But nobody ever knows it

You know it's kind of like this I aint feeling too well this morning, but you cannot tell, because I'm shining on the outside

I may feel a little down in my spirit, right now, but I am shouting on the outside

I may be pressed down, but not out, cast down but not forsaken, all because I burn on the inside but shine on the outside

Some people can't find JESUS, because we are not shining

How can they follow a light that will not even burn?

God can't use us if we aint going to shine

Beloved notice that when using a light bulb that if the bulb don't burn then it isn't any good

What God wants us to see today he will not use anyone that
will not burn on the inside?

Burn with conviction
Burn with deliverance
Burn with sense of healing
Burn with love
Burn with understanding
Burn with peace
Burn with salvation

But that's not all some of us are flickers
You know what I'm saying we have a light but it goes in and
out

Comes on Sunday morning
But flickers off come benediction

Comes on at funerals
But flickers off afterwards

Comes on at weddings
But flickers off during the after-party

Comes on during when we are in the hospital
But flickers off when we get healed

Comes on when we in trouble, but flickers off when we get out

But I got news for you; God wants you to keep you to keep
your light on

Saint Augustine says: "light passes through pollution but does
not become polluted"

You know that is the way that we ought to be

Pass through crack houses, but not be crack-heads

Pass through prostitutes-houses
But not changed over

Pass through underhanded situations, but remain upright

Pass through schemers but still shoot straight

We ought to be able to pass through without being polluted
why?

Because we are light of the world

Light is not made to be hid

It is made to be on a lamp stand so people can see you

Before I go I want you to see these things

You see the bulb is only the signal

You have to be connected to the conductor that carries the
electricity

Electricity cord which connects to the power source

This means that we are not the light we just carry the light

Tell somebody you better leave your light on . . .

This is M.E. Lyons and I'll leave the light on for you
I will not allow the enemy to turn out my light

I've Got Something In My Eye

Matthew 7:1-5

Our land is plagued with judging one another

Schools
Social relationships
Presidential campaign
(Use some current events)

But what is so sad is that judging has crept into the halls of
our churches

Have you ever known anybody whose frail and feeble minded
focus is always on you?

Seems like they are tickled to death just to pick on you

They always have something to say!

If you're too young; you lack experience
If you have gray hair, too old

We have become so supercilious, snobbish, and
condescending
That it is a shame

We find a microscope attempting to expose others
shortcomings when ours are on billboards

We have it bad talking about everybody

Some people only come to church just to get a report so they can go back home and spread the news

Brother this and that was asleep in church

Sister Do-nothing thought she really did it when she got up before the people

Pastor Not-a-lot preached but he didn't say anything

Just coming to get a report to run back and judge

(Story of Nathan telling David a story)

II Samuel 12:1-7
Nathan gave David a Visionary aid to assist him in understanding don't judge anybody until you are right

That's why David said Lord don't work on my neighbors I need you to work on me

Create in me

Restore unto me the joy

Then watch the systematic shift in David's testimony;

Then . . . I will teach transgressors Thy ways, and sinners will be converted to thee
(Psalms 51:12-19)

Tell somebody sitting close to you I have to take care of myself before I can help you with what you struggling with

I cannot talk about your tight dress until I take mines off;
I understand I might not have it on here but I had it on last
night

I can tell you to stop sagging when that's all I do is sag

I can't tell you to cover yourself up when I am exposed to the
world

Tell'em as a matter of fact I got something in my eye right now

Excuse me I need to get this out

Jesus told Peter I prayed for you now after you get converted
then you strengthen the brethren
(Luke22:32)

We are not log-toting speck inspectors

We are not to sit on the bench perpetrating to be

I just believe that some of us feel as though we have been
spiritually hired to judge other people

1st point
Watch your measuring stick
Verses 1 and 2

Judge in Greek means krin-ete which is translated criticize

I know we don't have anybody in this church that criticizes
but let me talk about somebody else

Whatever you do they criticize

Want to build a new church
Want to get a better car than what you had
Finally get married
Get a new suit
Buy a home that you are comfortable with

Ok let me come closer;

Start coming to church more often
Praising the Lord
Testifying

Usually what bothers us about somebody else is something
we don't like about ourselves

When you judge you are judged by that same measuring stick

A wise man said we need be careful because your judgment
will become your verdict

2nd point
Make sure you looking at what you are looking at
Verse 3

I know it's an oxymoron, but let me explain myself

When we close our eyes we actually see the inside of our
eyelids

Now watch this

Otherwise whenever we have a beam in our eye it causes us
to close our eyes and what we really see is ourselves

I guess what I really am trying to convey is that the only reason we can really tell if a person is phony is because we can attest to it ourselves

They don't amount to hill of beans

They are only doing to get what they want

They after the money

Their marriage aint going to last
How are they going to pay that note, it's not going to happen

Let me ask you a question

You know what a censor does don't you?

Censor bleeps out anything that someone doesn't want you to see or hear

3rd point
Take care of your own porch
Verse 4

Otherwise before you look at me look at yourself

Self righteousness turns into censoriousness, which produces false benevolence

That's when you hear people saying "Let me help you with that"

Who have you criticized this week?

This proverbial maxim needs to etched in every home somewhere where everybody can see it

Think about yourself first

You know the Williams brothers used to sing a song that said "sweep around your own front door before you try to sweep around mine"
(Galatians 6:1)

Even being prejudice is being judgmental

The root word of prejudice is judge

The prefix is pre

We need to stop stereotyping

You know when something is in your eye; whether it is a hair or dust, it causes you to see blurry

Makes you close your eyes

And if it stays to long it causes tears to come from your eyes

Are you hearing what I am saying?

All I'm saying is be careful how you judge because it just may come back on you the same way you put it out

Haman desired to hang Mordecai for standing up for his people

But the same gallows or hanging place he setup for Mordecai was the one they hung him with

(Esther 7:10)

Have I got a witness?

Adonizebek sent out a decree that 70 kings would have their big toes and thumbs cut off, but before he knew it they were after him and cut his off

When he says thou hypocrite let me give you a short lesson and I'm gone

Hypocrite is translated Greek as actor

Literally a second face; we call it being two-faced
Greek actors wore masks to represent the actor they portrayed

In order to take out a speck it is very delicate and difficult
There is nothing more sensitive in the body more than the eye

The instant we touch it closes

We have to be gentle to clean it out
Our spiritual eye is our soul

Nightmares

I Thessalonians 5:17

Many times in life we are encumbered with experiences that seem to come across as nightmares . . .

We live in homes whereas it feels as if we live in a nightmare . . .

Work on jobs that act as if they are nightmares . . .

Live next door to people who make our lives as nightmares . . .

Worship with people who make our lives a living nightmare . . .

But this day Paul helps us understand how to handle our nightmares . . .

I need to quickly suggest that you ought to be careful who you allow to pray for you as well . . .

Because sometimes the very people we have pray for us are people who have no fellowship with God . . .

How can you talk to a God you have no relationship with . . .

Dr AJ Jordan said: you can do more after you prayed; but you cannot do more until you pray . . .

Tell somebody you have to pray . . .

The reason most people live nightmares are due to the fact that some people suffer from PTSD-POST TRAUMATIC STRESS DISORDER . . .

You keep re-experiencing the event
Anxiety sets in
Sleeplessness
Dissociation

Two types one which last about a month . . .

Then there is the delayed . . . which is never dealt with . . . person uses defenses to cope with it . . .

Alcohol
Drugs
Immoral acts
Stepping on somebody else

Just to feel better about themselves . . .

So watch what Paul tells the Church at Thessalonica . . .
He starts in verse 16 by saying rejoice evermore . . .

There has to be a reason why rejoice evermore was placed before pray without ceasing . . . and notice it says evermore instead of forever . . .

Verse 16 says: rejoice . . .

Verse 18 says give thanks . . .

Verse 16 says go to bed rejoicing . . .

Verse 18 says get up with thanksgiving . . .

I know what you are saying I don't see that . . . stay with me . . .

You have to wonder why he begins with going to bed . . . well because evermore . . . *(Not forever)* in Greek means after . . .

After you have went through hell . . .
Talked about
Lied on
Done wrong
Stepped on
Looked over
Disrespected

Otherwise after your day is over . . . rejoice because it could have been worse . . .

After he says rejoice he moves onto our text . . . Pray without ceasing . . .

That's impossible . . . *(To the unbeliever . . .)*

How can you pray 24-7?

Whatever was on your mind when you went to bed will rest in your mind-your subconscious . . .

Eating the wrong thing can give you nightmares . . . watch what you eat . . .

It's like watching a scary movie and then going to bed . . .

What he is saying is we need to go to sleep with communication with Jesus . . .

Not . . . now I lay me down to sleep . . . you better talk to Him like you really need Him . . .

One Greek translation says pray without ceasing means . . . pray without intermission . . .

Intermission means a period when an action ceases . . .

Otherwise don't stop being who we are supposed to be . . .

I am going to lay my religion down . . .

God will understand . . . forgive . . .

Get this: in the middle of these scriptures is the word pray . . . Greek . . . PROSS . . .

Stay with me: this means to forward . . .
(Phone forwarding)

Are you still on the line or have you hung up on me?

If I could not get to the phone it was forwarded to somebody who could . . . we used to call it *72 . . .

I need about five people in here to just tell somebody who will hear you: when I can't get to the call I forward to HIM . . .

You better learn how to forward your calls . . . especially at night . . .

Well, when is night when I cannot handle the issues . . .

Just shout you better learn how to pray . . .

That's really all we do when we pray is forward our conversations to somebody who can handle them . . .

You need to know how to go to bed right . . .
I used to love watching a movie called "nightmare on elm street" . . .

They would sing a song periodically that was supposed to scare us . . .

1, 2, Freddy's coming for you . . . 3, 4, better lock the door . . .
But, with this scripture you can go to bed at night and not worry about thing . . .

You see God will intercept your problems . . . worries . . . concerns . . . issues . . .

Listen, in order to forward like we do . . . you would have to be at the current place where you wanted the calls transferred from . . .

Otherwise you have to learn how to pray for yourself . . .

But not only that you need to forward from the place where the nightmares are taking place . . .

How can you forward pray . . . in order to do so you have to have a constant subconscious-superego . . . like your breathing . . . walking . . .

But don't miss this: he then moves to in everything give thanks . . .

This will bless you if you let it . . .

The word thing in Greek means HY-MAIR-UH . . . which is derivative of HEM-I . . . which means to sit . . .

Ok, I have never known anyone to roll off the bed to stand up in the morning . . .

I never have known anyone to stand up in the bed in order to stand up . . .

We sit on the side of the bed . . .

And what Paul says is while you sit . . . give HIM thanks . . .

Why . . . because whilst we slept . . . He took care of our nightmares . . .

Thanksgiving ought to follow prayer . . .

Tell your neighbor: GOOD NIGHT . . .

If you don't understand . . .
Weeping may endure for a night . . .

But joy cometh in the morning . . . that's where we thank Him . . .

Go find about three people and encourage them and say: if you want to get rid of the nightmares . . . go to bed right . . .

You have to rejoice before bed . . .

Forward your calls . . .

But when you get up and sit . . . sit up with Thanksgiving . . .

When you do this . . . you can better understand how Jesus could go to bed in a storm . . .

Lastly let me share with you what verse 19 says . . .

Quench not the spirit . . .

Otherwise don't rejoice, pray, and thank him . . . then try to hold back when the Holy Spirit says

Run
Jump
Shout
Dance
Holler
Speak in tongues—in tongues is internally . . . use your prayer language . . . between you and God . . .

Don't extinguish what He is trying to ignite . . .

Acts 7:51 says: don't resist the Holy Spirit . . .

The Application of Illustrations

Illustrations are a tool that further explains how the Sermon/
Message is truly relevant and believable They should not be
a story that is antiquated and outdated that it does not connect
with the present situation Illustrations should be given a
twist of your personality and the changing of genders and
particulars help personalize the stories Doctor Joel Gregory;
one of the greatest minds of our time says: Illustrations should
be relevant and real (believable) This is so true, if they are not
believable to you it will not be believable to those listening
to you and especially if those who are listening know that it
is not a true story and out of your character If it is not a story
you have lived than present it as such. Rather use them for the
sake of integrity and it being an altruism; use them to build up
not to tear down.

God Is Real
Illustration:

There was a father and son who were sitting around one day talking and the son asked the father why is it that you believe in God? The father smiled and proceeded to answer but the son said: Daddy can you touch God the father said: no. The son said, well can you see God, the father said no. He then said well dad can you smell God, the father said no. The son laughing walked away and said then I rest my case. About a couple of hours later the father received a call that his son was in an accident. The father arrived at the hospital and walked into the room and checked to see how his son was doing and then asked his son how are you doing: the son said dad I am in pain. The father said well son, can you touch pain? The son said no. The father said well can you see pain, the son smiling said no. The father said can you smell pain; the son said daddy quit playing you know nobody can smell pain. The father then asked well how do you know that it's pain. The son said because I can feel pain. The father shouted with joy said; that is the same with me. I know God is real because I can feel Him.

The Things God Use
Illustration:

The story goes of a young boy who had a brother who always received everything he desired and one particular day he came home and his brother ran to his room and found all sorts of toys for him. He then ran over to his brother's room to see what he had received and started giggling and called for his brother to come upstairs and see his surprise. The younger brother ran upstairs with great anticipation and walked into his room and in the middle of the floor was pony manure and he ran and started jumping up and down in it and laughing. The older brother confused asked: why are you so happy? The baby brother said because if there is manure in my room there has to be a pony around here somewhere!

God's Protection
Illustration:

There was an elderly man who was walking home one night and a younger man ran up to him to rob him and while he was preparing to rob him; all of the sudden he ran away and not understanding the elderly gentleman went home and later that evening he was watching the news and seen the same young man on the news and had been arrested for robbing and killing a couple. Surprised the elderly gentlemen got up and told his wife he was going down to the jail to find out what happened. When he arrived he sat down to speak with the young man and asked him why didn't you rob me; why did you let me go? The young man said I had every intention of robbing you but three men showed up while I was trying to rob you. Startled the elderly gentlemen asked: well what did the one in front look like? Young man proceeded to say: well his eyes were like fire, his hair was kind of like wool, and he had a calming voice. The older man said: say no more I know who you are talking about; that's my Jesus and the two men on the sides of me were: grace and mercy!

It Is Not As Bad As It Seems
Illustration:

It was said that a man was given a horse and one of the horse's leg was broken and he became sickly. Later his horse died, and it was noised that a battalion was coming through town and drafting soldiers for a war and everyone who had a horse would be drafted. So when they showed up to this particular home they asked the man do you have a horse and he replied no; the sergeant said well that was the only way you could be exempted from the war. The truth is something's in life that seem bad are really for your benefit!

You Are Going Too Fast
Illustration:

The story of me and my wife LaTish driving with a flat and we were inching along a often traveled road and as we were passing a place over to our right she said I have never seen that before and I said it is amazing the things you see when you are going slow . . . and the truth is sometimes we are going too fast

FUNERAL ILLUSTRATIONS

It Should Have Killed Me
Application:

There was a woman who had visited her doctor and upon the doctor's findings; she said that she had a tumor and it needed to remove for any chance at a longer lifespan. So as the surgery had drawn to a close and the young lady was in her room she came around and asked the nurse if she could speak to the doctor. When the doctor arrived she asked her would you bring me my tumor. The doctor looking lost said: why do you need the tumor; we have never had this request before? She looked at the doctor and smiled and said: I want to see what was supposed to kill me!

This Is The Way
Application:

A young man was traveling to a family reunion and was lost and seen on the right side of the road a man sitting at an abandoned gas station and stopped to ask for directions. As he approached the man he said sir could you please tell me how to get to a family reunion at this particular address? He said yes sir, what you need to do is go down this hill, up the next, around the bend, through a rough rocky road, and you will run right into it. The young man knowing he was so close to seeing his long lost family members got in his car closed the door; went down the hill and up the next, around the bend and through the rough rocky path and ran into a cemetery. Disgusted that he had lost even more time he got out and said I am going back to ask this man why would he give me wrong directions. He got in his car and slammed the door went through the rocky path, around the bend, down the hill and up the next got out and walked to the man and said why would you give me the wrong directions? The older man said well did you follow my directions? He said yeah. Well where did it take you? He said to a cemetery! He said well I gave you the right directions; your problem is you didn't go through the cemetery because that is the way to family reunion. Isn't that how life is down and up around and through hard times and then to end up in the cemetery. The good news is there is a reunion but it is on the other side of the cemetery!

About the Author

Pastor M.E. Lyons has felt the calling of God on his life from his youth and was called into the Gospel Ministry in 1980 at the tender age of four, in the city of Rowlett, Texas at the Zion Missionary Baptist Church under the leadership of Rev. George Jackson, Jr., while he had indeed been called of God to preach the Word he also was entrusted with the natural gifting of playing music, but soon after realizing there was a call to move to utilizing the gift that had been deposited in other ministries he then began to accept the position of Minister of Music at Churches where his gifting was needed. In September of 2001 he realized the gifting that was molded and created for him in a wife and then married LaTish Luckey-Lyons and of this union are three children: Deja Z. Lyons, Myron E. Lyons, II, and Jeremiah Matthias Ezekiel Lyons.

To contact the Author:

Pastor ME Lyons
Email: melmanministries@gmailcom
Mobile: (214) 641-8115
Pastor's Office: (936) 634-6060

Mailing Address:
Attention: Pastor ME Lyons
751 Kilgore Drive 5a
Henderson, Texas 75652

Goodwill Missionary Baptist Church
812 East Lufkin Avenue
Lufkin, Texas 75901

Other Book(s) Written/Published:
Fresh Air Volume One
The Mind: The Pulpit of GOD
Fifty Two Weeks of Grace (Weekly Devotional Guide Edition One)
The testimony of the sheep . . . according to Psalms 23